**CHAMPION
SOCCER CLUBS**

D0479095

US WOMEN'S NATIONAL TEAM

SOCCER CHAMPIONS

JEFF SAVAGE

LERNER PUBLICATIONS ◆ MINNEAPOLIS

Lerner Publications Company
A division of Lerner Publishing Group, Inc.
241 First Avenue North
Minneapolis, MN 55401 USA

For reading levels and more information, look up this title at www.lernerbooks.com.

Main body text set in Adrianna Regular.
Typeface provided by Chank.

Library of Congress Cataloging-in-Publication Data

Names: Savage, Jeff, 1961– author.
Title: US Women's National Team : soccer champions / Jeff Savage.
Other titles: U.S. Women's National Team | United States Women's National Team
Description: Minneapolis : Lerner Publications, 2019. | Series: Champion soccer clubs | Includes bibliographical references and index. | Audience: Age 7–11. | Audience: Grade 4 to 6.
Identifiers: LCCN 2017044248 (print) | LCCN 2017052084 (ebook) | ISBN 9781541525542 (eb pdf) | ISBN 9781541519916 (lb : alk. paper) | ISBN 9781541527973 (pb : alk. paper)
Subjects: LCSH: U.S. Women's National Soccer Team—History—Juvenile literature. | Women soccer players—United States—Biography—Juvenile literature.
Classification: LCC GV944.U5 (ebook) | LCC GV944.U5 .S28 2019 (print) | DDC 796.3340973—dc23

LC record available at https://lccn.loc.gov/2017044248

Manufactured in the United States of America
1 - 44327 - 34573 - 1/9/2018

CONTENTS

INTRODUCTION

The final match of the 2015 **Women's World Cup** began with a bang. Three minutes into the game, US player Megan Rapinoe booted a **corner kick** to the front of the goal. Teammate Carli Lloyd raced forward and slammed the ball into the net. The US Women's National Team (USWNT) had a 1–0 lead against Japan.

The US women stayed on the attack. Lauren Holiday passed the ball into the **penalty area**. Julie Johnston pushed it forward, and Lloyd drilled a shot to make the score 2–0. The USWNT fans in the crowd cheered and danced.

Carli Lloyd won the US Soccer Player of the Year award in 2008 and 2015.

USWNT fans made a lot of noise during the 2015 final match to support their soccer heroes.

More than 50,000 people filled BC Place in Vancouver, Canada. Thousands of USWNT fans had traveled there to see the final match against Japan. About 25 million people viewed the game on television. It was the most watched soccer match in US history.

The Women's World Cup takes place every four years. The USWNT had won the tournament twice in the past, but 2015 marked 16 years since their last championship. In 2011, they lost the final match to Japan in a **shoot-out**. The USWNT were determined not to lose this time.

At the 2015 Women's World Cup, the USWNT did not allow a goal against them for 540 minutes. No team in tournament history had gone longer without allowing a goal.

A Japanese defender sent a **header** into the air. The ball fell near her goal. Holiday smashed it into the upper-right corner of the net for a 3–0 US lead.

Two minutes later, the USWNT struck again. Lloyd had the ball in the middle of the field. She sidestepped a defender and blasted a long shot. It traveled more than 150 feet (46 m). Japan's goalie couldn't reach it. The ball bounced into the goal, setting off a wild US celebration. Lloyd had scored the first **hat trick** in a Women's World Cup final match. After the game, US coach Jill Ellis called Lloyd "unbelievable" and a "rock star."

Japan scored twice to cut the lead in half. But US **midfielder** Tobin Heath knocked in a pass from Morgan Brian to seal the victory, 5–2. It was the highest-scoring title game in Women's World Cup history.

The USWNT and their fans celebrated. US stars Abby Wambach and Christie Rampone lifted the Women's World Cup trophy with their teammates. "It doesn't feel real," Lloyd said. "We just made history."

JOHNSTON
4
SECRETARY OF DEFENSE

USWNT players celebrate another goal against Japan. Other than the United States, only Germany has won the Women's World Cup more than once.

1 BURSTING ON THE SCENE

Soccer has always been more popular in places
such as Europe and South America than in the
United States. Yet late in the 20th century, soccer's
popularity grew in the United States. That was
especially true for women and girls. In 1976, less than
10 percent of high school soccer players were girls.
By 1990, the percentage jumped to 35 percent. Amid

this growth, the US Women's National Team formed in 1985. The team played four games its first year. They didn't win any of them.

Anson Dorrance became the team's coach the next year. Dorrance had led the University of North Carolina women's soccer team to three national titles. He turned the US team into winners too. The USWNT won four of six games in 1986.

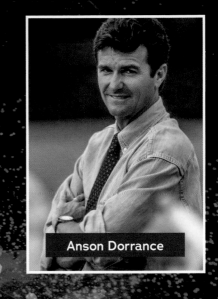

Anson Dorrance

Mia Hamm (*center*) held the record for 14 years for most goals scored in international matches. US player Abby Wambach took the record from Hamm in 2013.

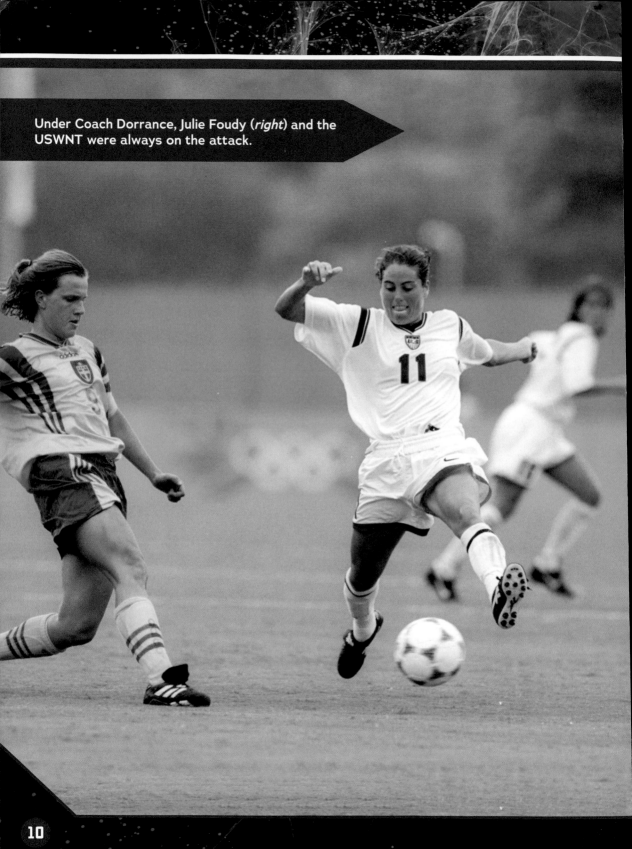

Under Coach Dorrance, Julie Foudy (*right*) and the USWNT were always on the attack.

The USWNT played with an aggressive style that was new to the women's game. "We were gritty," said Dorrance. "We were different and we scared teams because we were different."

The Women's World Cup started in 1991. The US beat Norway in the final match to win the tournament.

Women's soccer was included in the Olympic Games for the first time in 1996, in Atlanta, Georgia. The USWNT cruised through the **knockout stage** to meet China for the gold medal.

More than 76,000 fans filled the stands to watch the gold medal game. Shannon MacMillan and Tiffeny Milbrett scored for the United States in a 2–1 triumph.

USWNT players celebrate after the gold medal match at the 1996 Olympics.

Brandi Chastain's celebration after helping the USWNT win the 1999 Women's World Cup became famous with soccer fans everywhere.

2 REACHING THE TOP

The 1999 Women's World Cup played out in stadiums across the United States. The USWNT used their home-field advantage to reach the final match against China. About 90,000 fans packed the Rose Bowl in Pasadena, California.

The teams battled to a 0–0 tie. The intense contest came down to a shoot-out. US goalkeeper

Briana Scurry stopped the third shot from China. The crowd roared.

Scurry's save gave the United States a chance to win it. Brandi Chastain blasted in the winning shot. She fell to her knees and ripped off her jersey during a wild celebration.

The USWNT had become extremely popular. They appeared on the cover of magazines and visited the White House. The United States finished second in the 2000 Olympics and third in the 2003 Women's World Cup. Many teams

USWNT players were honored at the White House after winning the 1999 Women's World Cup.

would be happy with such results. Yet for the USWNT, second and third wasn't good enough.

In 2004, the USWNT won the Olympics again. Abby Wambach's goal in the final match against Brazil sealed the gold medal. At the 2007 Women's World Cup, US goalie Hope Solo had three **shutouts**. Fans were surprised when Coach Greg Ryan replaced Solo with Scurry for the next match. Brazil crushed the United States, 4–0. It was the biggest loss ever for the USWNT. The team soon fired Coach Ryan.

Abby Wambach celebrates her goal against Brazil in the gold medal match of the 2004 Olympic Games. Wambach led the team with four goals in the tournament.

The USWNT made up for their 2007 loss to Brazil by beating them in the 2008 Olympic Games, 1–0.

By 2008, Carli Lloyd had become a scoring star. The team captured gold at the 2008 Olympic Games when she scored in the 96th minute. Lloyd scored both US goals in the gold medal match at the 2012 Olympics. Then her heroics at the 2015 World Cup helped keep the US women on top.

Carli Lloyd's header during the 2012 Olympic gold medal match against Japan streaked into the right side of the goal. The score came just eight minutes into the game, and Lloyd would score again later to secure the win.

USWNT TIMELINE

1985 The team forms.

1991 They win the first Women's World Cup.

1996 They win the Olympic gold medal for the first time.

1999 They win the Women's World Cup for the second time.

2004 They win the Olympic gold medal for the second time.

2008 They win the Olympic gold medal for the third time.

2012 They win the Olympic gold medal for the fourth time.

2015 They win the Women's World Cup for the third time.

2017 They finish second in the first Tournament of Nations event.

The heroes of the USWNT wave to fans at the Canyon of Heroes in 2015.

3 THE NEW HEROES

The USWNT is beloved by soccer fans in the United States. After their 2015 Women's World Cup win, the team took part in a parade in New York City. It went down a section of Broadway known as the Canyon of Heroes, where people have honored athletes and others for many years. It was the first parade in honor of a women's soccer team along that route.

There are about 20 members of the USWNT. They practice at the Olympic Training Center in California. When they don't have national team duties, many of the women play in **pro** leagues around the world.

USWNT members work hard for their country. Jill Ellis knows how to get the most out of her players. Through 2016, she had

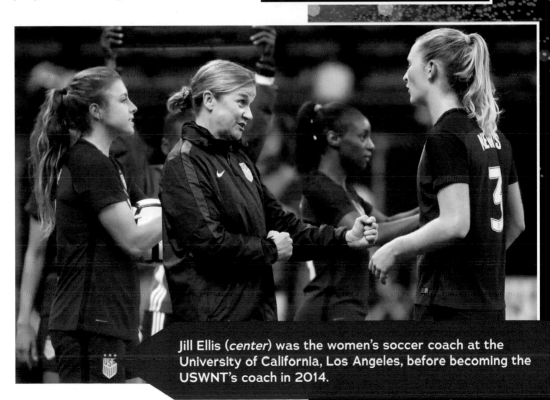

Jill Ellis (*center*) was the women's soccer coach at the University of California, Los Angeles, before becoming the USWNT's coach in 2014.

coached 74 USWNT games and lost just three. She is the only US soccer coach to win the World Coach of the Year award.

Ellis knows that second place isn't good enough. She expects the United States to keep winning soccer's biggest prizes. She says, "The thing about reaching the top of a mountain is that there's always another one to climb."

Christen Press (*center*) played soccer at Stanford University and became the team's all-time leading scorer. She joined the USWNT in 2012.

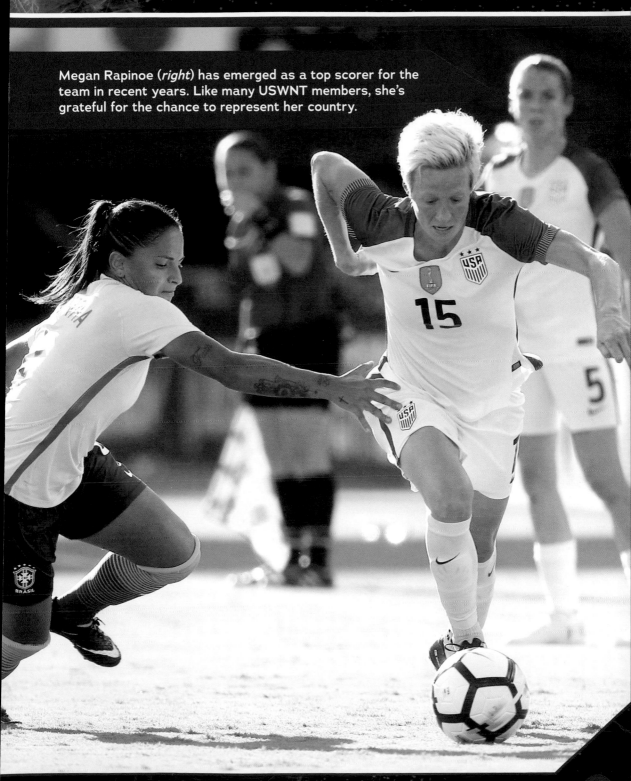

Megan Rapinoe (*right*) has emerged as a top scorer for the team in recent years. Like many USWNT members, she's grateful for the chance to represent her country.

4 USWNT

SUPER

STARS

Millions of girls play youth soccer in the United States each year. Many of them want to play on the USWNT when they're older. With that much competition, winning a place on the team is quite an accomplishment. Here are some of the best players in USWNT history.

MICHELLE AKERS [1985–2000]

In 1985, Michelle Akers scored the first goal in USWNT history. She was the leading scorer in the first Women's World Cup with 10 goals in six games. Her fierce style of play resulted in more than a dozen surgeries to repair knee injuries. She retired from soccer to rescue horses and other animals at her farm in Georgia.

JULIE FOUDY [1987–2004]

Julie Foudy attended Stanford University's medical school, but her goals changed in college. She focused on soccer and became the USWNT captain for 14 years. Since leaving the team, she appears on TV as a soccer expert and works to advance women's rights.

MIA HAMM [1987–2004]

Maybe the team's most popular player ever, Mia Hamm was the face of the USWNT for years. Before joining the national team, she led the University of North Carolina to four straight national college championships. FIFA (Fédération Internationale de Football Association), which oversees international soccer, named her World Player of the Year in 2001 and 2002.

KRISTINE LILLY [1987–2010]

Kristine Lilly joined the national team while she was still in high school. In 1995, she competed against men as the only woman in a professional indoor soccer league. She played in 354 USWNT games, by far the most in team history. Lilly is the only player in international women's soccer to have played in four different decades and five World Cups.

ABBY WAMBACH [2001–2015]

US fans loved Abby Wambach's fearless attacks and diving headers. She was tall and strong, which made her almost impossible to stop when the ball was in the air. US Soccer named her Female Athlete of the Year in 2003, 2004, 2007, 2010, 2011, and 2013.

In 2013, she became the all-time leading scorer in international soccer. Her 184 goals are more than any woman or man has scored.

HOPE SOLO [2005–2016]

Goalkeeper Hope Solo's stats are amazing. She had more **caps** (202), wins (153), and shutouts (102) than any other goalie in USWNT history. In her first year with the team in 2005, she started seven games and had seven shutouts. She's active off the field too. Solo ran in the Chicago Marathon to raise money for charity and even competed on the TV show *Dancing with the Stars*.

CARLI LLOYD (2005–PRESENT)

Carli Lloyd has been the USWNT's best goal scorer in the biggest moments in recent years. She scored the gold medal–winning goals in both the 2008 and 2012 Olympic Games. Her hat trick in the 2015 World Cup final match against Japan put the USWNT over the top. In 2015, she became the third US player to win the Best FIFA Women's Player award, and she won it again in 2016.

MEGAN RAPINOE (2006–PRESENT)

USWNT star Megan Rapinoe has moved all around the world to play soccer. She played for teams in Australia and France before returning to the United States and joining the Seattle Reign. Rapinoe is one of the USWNT's most skilled scorers and has come up with huge goals in the Olympics and Women's World Cup.

STATS STORY

The USWNT has been the most successful national team in the world since they took international soccer by storm in the mid-1980s. They've had many incredible performances over the years. Here are some of the team's most amazing statistics:

- **MOST CAREER GOALS:** ABBY WAMBACH (184)

- **MOST CAREER HAT TRICKS:** MIA HAMM (10)

- **MOST CAREER ASSISTS:** MIA HAMM (145)

- **MOST CAREER WINS BY A GOALKEEPER:** HOPE SOLO (152)

- **MOST GOALS IN A SEASON:** MICHELLE AKERS (39)

- **WORLD CUP TITLES:** 3 (1991, 1999, 2015)

- **OLYMPIC GOLD MEDALS:** 4 (1996, 2004, 2008, 2012)

SOURCE NOTES

6   Steve Almasy, "Women's World Cup: Lloyd's Hat-Trick Leads U.S. to Third Title," *CNN*, July 6, 2015, http://edition.cnn.com/2015/07/05/football /womens-world-cup-final/index.html.

6   Ibid.

11   John D. Halloran, "The Rise and Rise of the United States Women's National Team," *Bleacher Report*, April 23, 2013, http://bleacherreport.com/articles /1614739-the-rise-and-rise-of-the-united-states-womens-national-team.

20   "On the Road to Rio," U.S. Soccer, accessed October 1, 2017, http://www .ussoccer.com/womens-national-team/about-the-wnt.

GLOSSARY

caps: international soccer matches played

corner kick: a kick from one of the corners of the field

hat trick: three goals scored by one player in a game

header: a shot or pass made with the head

knockout stage: the second part of the Women's World Cup in which match winners advance and losers are out of the tournament

midfielder: a soccer player who usually stays in the middle of the field between the forwards and the defenders

penalty area: an area in front of each goal. If a player on the defending team commits a penalty in the area, the other team gets a penalty shot.

pro: something done for money that other people do for fun

shoot-out: a series of five shots per team to determine the winner of a match

shutouts: games in which one team does not score

Women's World Cup: a tournament held every four years between the world's top national teams

FURTHER INFORMATION

Braun, Eric. *Incredible Sports Trivia: Fun Facts and Quizzes.* Minneapolis: Lerner Publications, 2018.

FIFA Women's World Cup France 2019
http://www.fifa.com/womensworldcup/index.html

Fishman, Jon M. *Abby Wambach.* Minneapolis: Lerner Publications, 2014.

Jökulsson, Illugi. *U.S. Women's Team: Soccer Champions!* New York: Abbeville, 2015.

National Women's Soccer League
http://www.nwslsoccer.com

USWNT—U.S. Soccer
https://www.ussoccer.com/womens-national-team#tab-1

INDEX

PHOTO ACKNOWLEDGMENTS

The images in this book are used with the permission of: Design elements: Lawkeeper/Shutterstock.com; sakkmesterke/Shutterstock.com; Michal Zduniak/Shutterstock.com; somchaij/Shutterstock.com; Content: Ben Radford/Corbis/Getty Images, pp. 4, 27 (top); The Asahi Shimbun/Getty Images, p. 5; Stuart Franklin/FIFA/Getty Images, p. 7; TOMMY CHENG/AFP/Getty Images, pp. 8, 9 (bottom); David Madison/Getty Images, p. 9 (top); Stephen Dunn/Getty Images, p. 10; Gilbert Iundt/Corbis/Getty Images, p. 11; ROBERTO SCHMIDT/AFP/Getty Images, p. 12; Vincent Laforet/Getty Images, p. 13; Ron Antonelli/NY Daily News Archive/Getty Images, p. 14; DANIEL GARCIA/AFP/Getty Images, p. 15; Jamie Squire/Getty Images, p. 16; lev radin/Shutterstock.com, p. 18; Chris Graythen/Getty Images, p. 19; Harry How/Getty Images, p. 20; Sean M. Haffey/Getty Images, p. 21; EFKS/Shutterstock.com, pp. 22–23; Allsport/Getty Images, p. 24 (top); Shaun Botterill/Getty Images, p. 24 (bottom); Rick Stewart/Allsport/Getty Images, p. 25 (top); Tony Duffy /Allsport/Getty Images, p. 25 (bottom); Richard Schultz/WireImage/Getty Images, p. 26 (top); Jonathan Daniel/Getty Images, p. 26 (bottom); Matthew Stockman/Getty Images, p. 27 (bottom).

Front cover: Jamie Sabau/Getty Images; Ezra Shaw/Getty Images; Matthew Visinsky/Icon Sportswire/Getty Images.